Dorothy Vaughan

Published in the United States of America by Cherry Lake Publishing
Ann Arbor, Michigan
www.cherrylakepublishing.com

Content Adviser: Ryan Emery Hughes, Doctoral Student, School of Education, University of Michigan
Reading Adviser: Marla Conn MS, Ed., Literacy specialist, Read-Ability, Inc.
Book Design: Jennifer Wahi
Illustrator: Jeff Bane

Photo Credits: © TommyBrison/Shutterstock, 5; © bioraven/Shutterstock, 7; © Courtesy of Vaughan Family/
Wikimedia, 9; © Jack Delano / Library of Congress, 11, 22; © Courtesy of Vaughan Family, 13; © NASA, 15;
© NASA, 17, 23; © sabrisy/Shutterstock, 19; © NASA, 21; Cover, 10, 14, 16, Jeff Bane; Various frames throughout,
© Shutterstock Images

Library of Congress Cataloging-in-Publication Data

Names: Loh-Hagan, Virginia, author.
Title: Dorothy Vaughan / by Virginia Loh-Hagan.
Other titles: My itty-bitty bio.
Description: Ann Arbor, MI : Cherry Lake Publishing, [2018] | Series: My
   itty-bitty bio | Audience: K to grade 3. | Includes index.
Identifiers: LCCN 2017031857| ISBN 9781534107113 (hardcover) | ISBN
   9781534108103 (pbk.) | ISBN 9781534109094 (pdf) | ISBN 9781534120082
   (hosted ebook)
Subjects: LCSH: Vaughan, Dorothy, 1910-2008--Juvenile literature. | United
   States. National Aeronautics and Space Administration--Biography--Juvenile
   literature. | African American women mathematicians--Biography--Juvenile
   literature. | Women mathematicians--Biography--Juvenile literature. |
   African American women--Juvenile literature.
Classification: LCC QA29.V32 L64 2018 | DDC 510.92 [B] --dc23
LC record available at https://lccn.loc.gov/2017031857

Printed in the United States of America
Corporate Graphics

About the author: Dr. Virginia Loh-Hagan is an author, university professor, former classroom teacher, and curriculum designer. She loves being the boss. Like Dorothy, she wants to make the changes that she can make and endure the things that she can't change. She lives in San Diego with her very tall husband and very naughty dogs. To learn more about her, visit: www.virginialoh.com

About the illustrator: Jeff Bane and his two business partners own a studio along the American River in Folsom, California, home of the 1849 Gold Rush. When Jeff's not sketching or illustrating for clients, he's either swimming or kayaking in the river to relax.

I was born in Missouri. It was 1910.

I finished college. I was 19.
I learned math.

What do you want to learn?

I got married. I had six children.

I taught math.

The United States had a **space program**. I was hired to work for it.

Blacks worked in one area. Whites worked in another. It was unfair.

How do you treat people fairly?

I led a group. We were black women.

We did math. We were called "human **computers**."

13

We did good work. We figured out flight **paths**.

We sent people into space.

I was a good leader. I was the program's first black boss.

Most bosses were white. Most were men.

Our space program became **NASA**. I **coded**. I was an expert **programmer**.

I taught others. Black women are smart. I wanted everyone to know that.

What can you teach others?

I died in 2008. I fought for blacks. I fought for women.

I changed what I could.

What would you like to ask me?

1943

1910

Born
1910

1949

2010

Died
2008

glossary

coded (KOH-did) told a computer how to do something

computers (kuhm-PYOO-turz) machines that can do really hard math problems; people who can do this are called "human computers"

NASA (NASS-uh) the National Aeronautics and Space Administration; it is in charge of the United States' space program

paths (PATHS) the ways something will travel to and in space

programmer (PROH-gram-ur) a person whose job is to give a computer directions that make it work a certain way

space program (SPAYS PROH-gram) a group that plans trips and activities into space

index